LANDMARK LEADERS:

Trailblazers Who Shaped History

I am becoming the best
version of myself.

LANDMARK
LEADERS:
Trailblazers Who Shaped History

Author:
Shawn Alexis Meekins

Derivative drawings from photography:
Shawn Alexis Meekins

Design:
Shawn Alexis Meekins

Editor:
Tamara Meekins
Laiyah Meekins
London Meekins

Library of Congress Control Number:
2026909310

This book was created to inspire kids to dream big and become leaders. The heroes before us worked hard and achieved amazing things. Their stories remind us that we can keep moving forward too. Inside each of us is a trailblazer ready to shine!

CONTENTS:

Katherine Johnson........................ 4
Neil deGrasse Tyson..................... 6
Mae C. Jemison.......................... 8
Harriet Tubman 10
Frederick Douglass 12
Booker T. Washington 14
Ida B. Wells 16
Mary McLeod Bethune 18
Rosa Louise McCauley Parks 20
Sylvia Mendez........................... 22
Dolores Huerta 24
Fannie Lou Hamer 26
Shirley Chisholm 28
Thurgood Marshall 30
Ketanji Brown Jackson 32
Nelson Mandela 34
Barack Obama 36
more amazing facts.....................38- 47

Katherine JOHNSON

Mathematician

Katherine Johnson was a brilliant mathematician who worked for NASA. She used her math skills to help send astronauts into space and bring them home safely. She worked at NASA for 33 years and was one of the first African American women to work there as a scientist. Katherine helped make big changes by showing how important smart, hard-working women could be in space science.

Johnson received the Presidential Medal of Freedom in 2015 from President Barack Obama.

Born in White Sulphur Springs, West Virginia, United States
August 26, 1918 -
February 24, 2020
Fun Fact:
Katherine's math helped launch the first American astronaut into orbit — and she did it all by hand before computers were common!

Neil deGrasse TYSON

Astrophysicist

Neil deGrasse Tyson is a famous scientist and space expert who helps people understand the universe. He talks about stars, planets, and space on TV and in books, making science fun and easy to learn. Mr. Tyson works at the Hayden Planetarium in New York City and loves sharing his excitement about space with everyone.

Tyson was accepted to Cornell University at the age of 17.

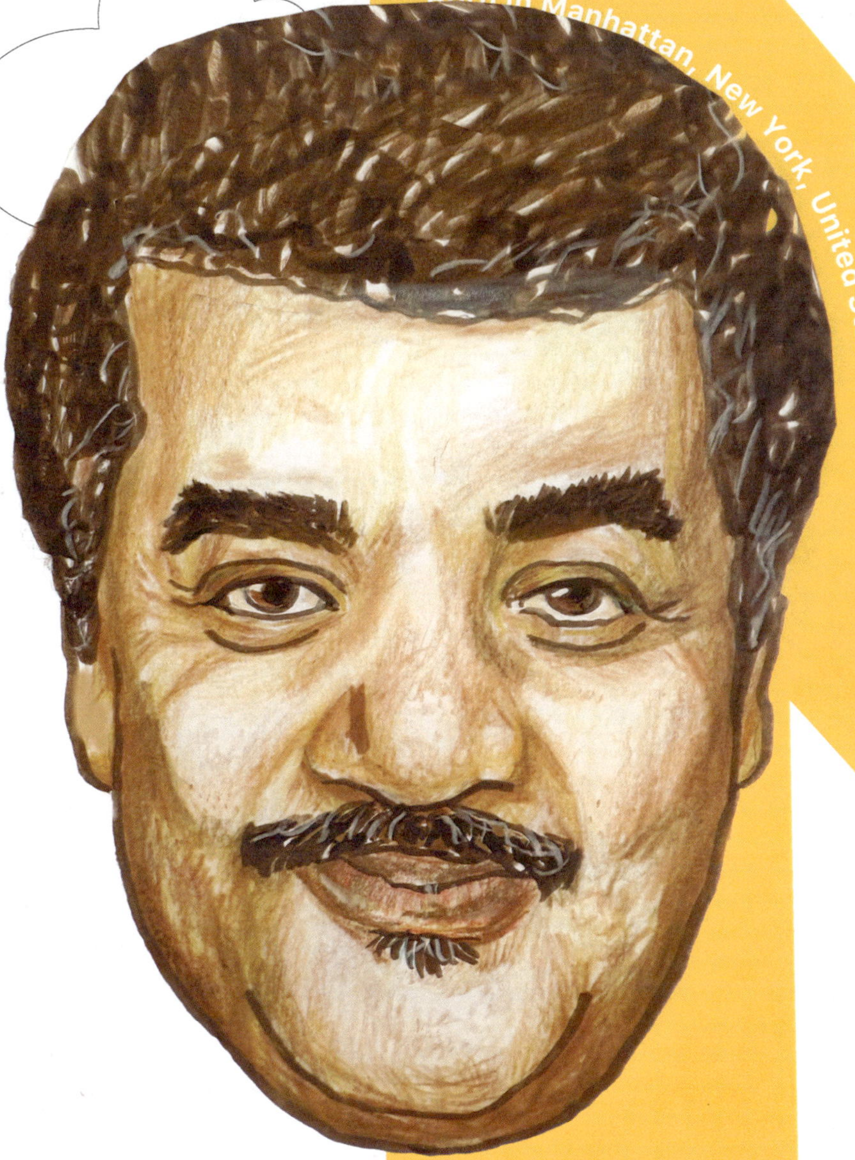

Born in Manhattan, New York, United States

October 5, 1958

Fun Fact:
Neil deGrasse Tyson once appeared on a popular TV show called "The Big Bang Theory" and even helped explain science on the show!

Mae Carol JEMISON

Americane Engineer, Physician, and NASA Astronaut

Mae C. Jemison is an engineer, doctor, and astronaut. In 1992, she became the first African American woman to travel into space when she flew on the Space Shuttle Endeavor. Mae inspires many people to dream big and explore the stars.

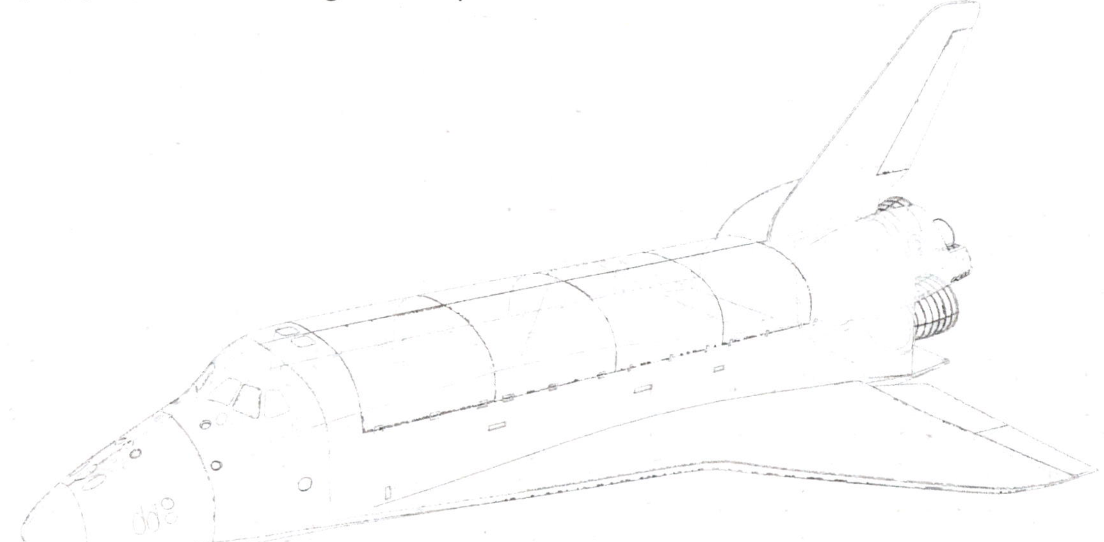

Born in Decatur, Alabama, United States
October 17, 1956
Fun Fact:
Mae Jemison not only became the first African American woman in space, but she also appeared in an episode of Star Trek: The Next Generation, fulfilling her childhood dream of being like the astronauts she saw on TV!

Harriet
TUBMAN

Birth name: Araminta "Minty" Ross

American Abolitionist and Social Activist

Harriet Tubman was a brave leader who helped many enslaved people escape to freedom through a secret network called the Underground Railroad. She risked her life many times to guide others to safety and became known as the "Moses of her people."

Harriett Tubman served in the Civil War as a cook, nurse, scout, and spy.

March 1822 –
March 10, 1913

Fun Fact:
Harriet Tubman made at least 13 trips back to the South and helped free about 70 people!

Fredrick
DOUGLASS

American Abolitionist and Orator

Frederick Douglass was a powerful speaker, writer, and leader who fought to end slavery and gain equal rights for African Americans. Born into slavery, he escaped and used his voice to change the country during the 1800s.

Born in Cordova, MD, United States
February 1818 - February 20, 1895
Fun Fact:
Frederick Douglass taught himself to read and write even though it was against the law for enslaved people to learn!

Booker T. WASHINGTON

American Educator and Author

Booker T. Washington was a well-known African American teacher, writer, and speaker. From the late 1800s to the early 1900s, he was one of the most important leaders in the Black community and worked hard to help African Americans get a better education and more opportunities.

The Tuskegee Institute 1881

Booker T. Washington's autobiography, *Up From Slavery*, was published in 1901 and became a bestseller.

April 5, 1856 –
November 14, 1915

Born in Hale's Ford, Westlake Corner, VA, United States

Fun Fact:
Booker T. Washington founded the
Tuskegee Normal and Industrial
Institute, which is now known as
Tuskegee University.

Ida Bell
WELLS

American Journalist and Sociologist

Ida B. Wells was a brave journalist and teacher who helped fight for civil rights. She worked hard to tell the truth about unfair treatment and helped start the NAACP, a group that works to protect the rights of Black people.

Fun Fact:
Ida B. Wells used her writing to speak out against injustice, even when it was dangerous to do so!

Mary McLeod
BETHUNE

American Educator and Philanthropist

Mary McLeod Bethune was a teacher, helper, and leader who worked to improve the lives of African American women and girls. She started the National Council of Negro Women to support women and created a magazine to share their stories and ideas.

The Daytona Education and Industrial Training school for Negro Girls building was established in 1904.

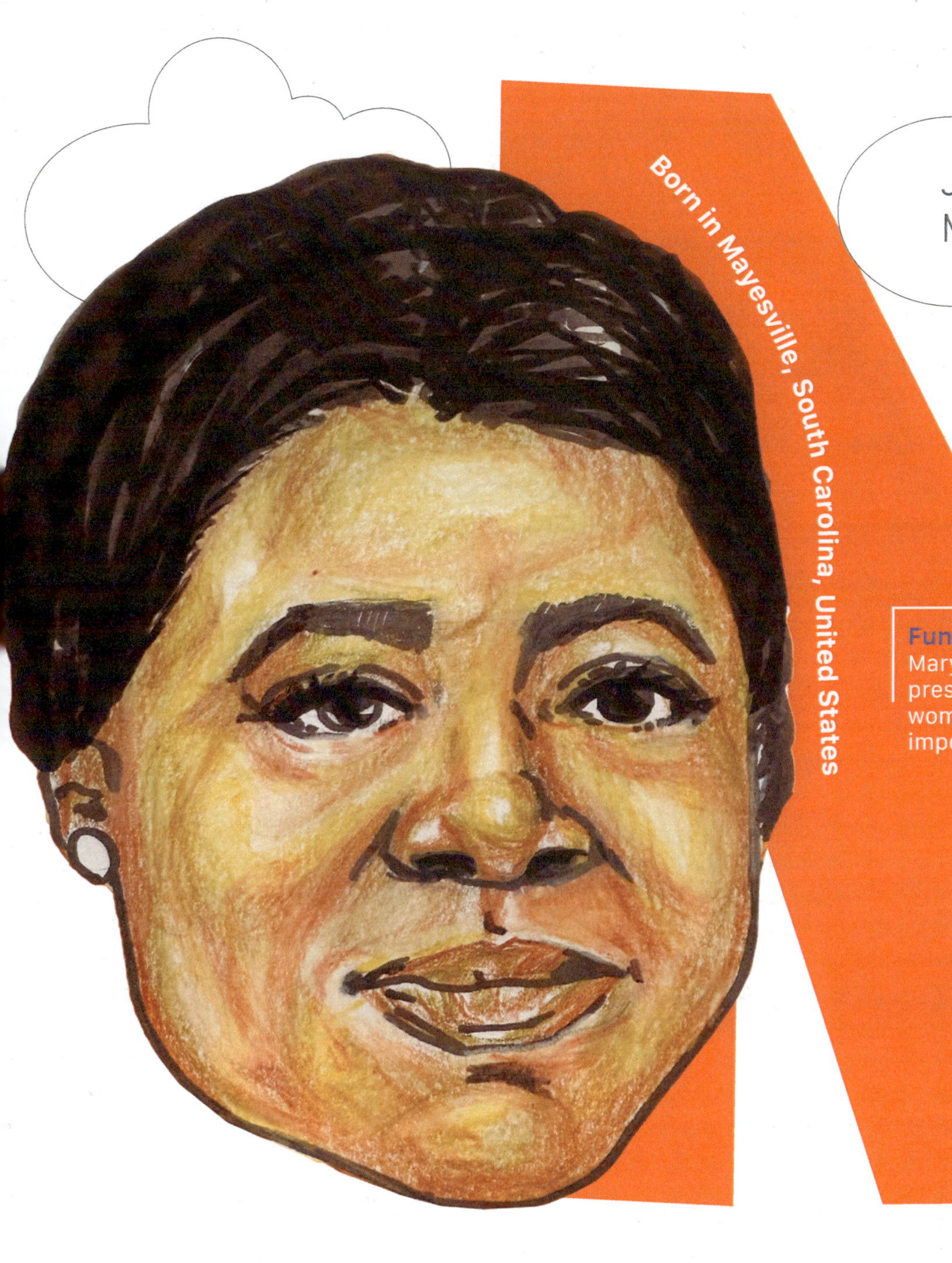

July 10, 1875 –
May 18, 1955

Fun Fact:
Mary Bethune advised several U.S. presidents and helped make sure women's voices were heard in important decisions!

Rosa
PARKS

Rosa Louise McCauley Parks was an important leader in the fight for civil rights. She is most famous for refusing to give up her seat to a white passenger on a bus in Montgomery, Alabama. Her brave action helped start the Montgomery Bus Boycott, a major event in the fight against unfair segregation laws.

The Montgomery Bus boycott lasted for 381 days

Born in Tuskegee, Alabama, United States
February 4, 1913 - October 24, 2005
Fun Fact:
Did you know Rosa Parks loved reading adventure stories and was a big fan of mystery novels?

Sylvia MENDEZ

American Civil Rights Activist and Retired Nurse

Sylvia Mendez is a civil rights hero who made history when she was only eight years old! She and her family helped win a big court case called Mendez v. Westminster in 1946. That case helped stop school segregation in California and helped start big changes across the country.

Los Angeles Times

February 19, 1946

RULING GIVES MEXICAN CHILDREN EQUAL RIGHTS

June 7, 1936
Born in Santa Ana, CA, United States
Fun Fact:
Sylvia Mendez was awarded the Presidential Medal of Freedom in 2011 — and her family's court case was even featured on a U.S. postage stamp in 2007!

I will stand up for my community like...

Dolores
HUERTA

American Labor Leader

Dolores Huerta is a community leader and activist who has spent her life fighting for the rights of farm workers and workers everywhere. She helped start the United Farm Workers union with Cesar Chavez and worked hard to bring fair treatment and better pay to farm workers across the country.

Fun Fact: When Dolores Huerta won a prize called the Puffin/Nation Prize for Creative Citizenship, she didn't keep the money — she used it to start the Dolores Huerta foundation in 2002, where people work together to make their communities stronger and fairer.

Born in Dawson, New Mexico, United States
April 10, 1930
Fun Fact:
Dolores Huerta once told people to "Sí, se puede," which means "Yes, we can!" and this phrase became a powerful message for many movements.

Fannie Lou HAMER

American Activist

Fannie Lou Hamer was a leader who fought for voting rights and women's rights. She worked to make sure everyone could vote and helped organize people to stand up for fairness. Fannie Lou was a vice-chair of the Freedom Democratic Party and spoke at an important meeting in 1964 to demand equal rights.

MISSISSIPPI FREEDOM DEMOCRATIC PARTY

Fun Fact: The Fannie Lou Hamer Cancer Foundation has helped thousands of women in Mississippi get free health check-ups. These check-ups, like mammograms, can find cancer early and help save lives!

October 6, 1917 -
March 14, 1977
Born in Montgomery County, MS, United States
Fun Fact:
Fannie Lou Hamer is famous for saying, "I'm sick and tired of being sick and tired," showing how determined she was to make change!

Shirley
CHISHOLM

First Black Congresswoman / Trailblazing Politician

Shirley Chisholm was a brave and bold leader who made history many times. In 1968, she became the first Black woman elected to the U.S. Congress. She represented Brooklyn, New York, for 14 years. In 1972, she became the first Black person and the first woman to run for President in the Democratic Party.

United States Capitol

November 30, 1924 -
January 1, 2005
Born in Brooklyn, New York, United States
Fun Fact:
Shirley's campaign slogan was "Unbought and Unbossed" and she truly lived by it!

Thurgood MARSHALL

Lawyer and former Solicitor General of the United States

Thurgood Marshall was a lawyer who fought for civil rights and became the first Black justice on the United States Supreme Court. He worked to make sure that everyone was treated fairly under the law and helped change unfair rules in America.

The Supreme Court Building

July 2, 1908 –
January 24, 1993

Fun Fact:
Before joining the Supreme Court, Thurgood Marshall won a famous case called Brown v. Board of Education, which helped end segregation in schools!

Ketanji Brown
JACKSON

Lawyer and former Solicitor General of the United States

Ketanji Brown Jackson is a lawyer and judge who made history by becoming the first Black woman to serve on the United States Supreme Court. The Supreme Court is the highest court in the country, where big decisions are made about laws and people's rights.

The Supreme Court Building

Sept 14, 1970
Born in Washington, DC, United States
Fun Fact:
When Ketanji was in high school, she was voted "Most Likely to Succeed" and she sure did by becoming a Supreme Court Justice!

Nelson MANDELA

Activist and former President of South Africa

Nelson Mandela was a South African leader who fought against apartheid, a system that treated people unfairly because of their skin color. In 1994, he became the first Black president of South Africa, elected by all the people in a fair election. As president, he worked hard to bring people together and end the problems caused by apartheid. Mandela was also the leader of the African National Congress, a group that worked for freedom and equality.

July 18, 1918 -
December 5, 2013

Fun Fact:
Mandela's Xhosa name, Rolihlahla, means "pulling the branch of a tree," which is a way of saying "troublemaker" but in a good way!

"Madiba" is a special family name from the Thembu people. It's the name of the clan that Nelson Mandela belonged to, and many people lovingly called him Madiba as a sign of respect.

Barack H. OBAMA

44th U.S. President
Nobel Peace Prize Winner 2009

Barack Obama was the 44th President of the United States and the first African American to ever hold that office. He served from 2009 to 2017 and worked to bring people together, improve healthcare, and create more opportunities for everyone.

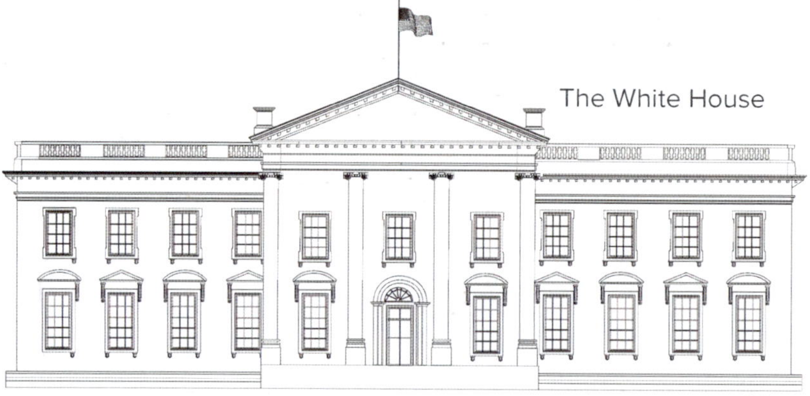

The White House

Fun Fact: At the Obama Presidential Center in Chicago, there is a giant wall called the "Power of Words." It's 88 feet tall and covered with inspiring quotes to remind people how powerful words can be!

Born in Hawaii, United States
August 4, 1961
Fun Fact:
Before becoming president, Obama was a lawyer, teacher, and U.S. Senator and he won a Grammy Award for narrating his own audiobook!

I will be...
THE GREATEST
VERSION OF
ME
courageous
determined
happy
brilliant
loving
intelligent
caring

I can make a positive
difference in the world

I am proud of my accomplishments

I am strong and capable

I Know My Self-worth

I believe in myself

I am enough

Love space, science experiments, or building awesome STEM toys? You might be the next great scientist, engineer, or astronaut!

Scientists explore new ideas, engineers build amazing solutions, and astronauts travel beyond Earth to discover what's out there.

What will you discover one day?

STEPHANIE WILSON

MAE CAROL JEMISON

JOAN HIGGINBOTHAM

DR. ELLEN OCHOA

DR. SIAN PROCTOR

JEANETTE EPPS

YVONNE DARLENE CAGLE

Do you love creating your own style, picking out cool outfits, or mixing fabrics and colors in fun ways? Do you ever imagine designing clothes that everyone wants to wear? You might be a future fashion designer!

Fashion designers use creativity and bold ideas to turn fabric into art people can wear. What kind of style would you create?

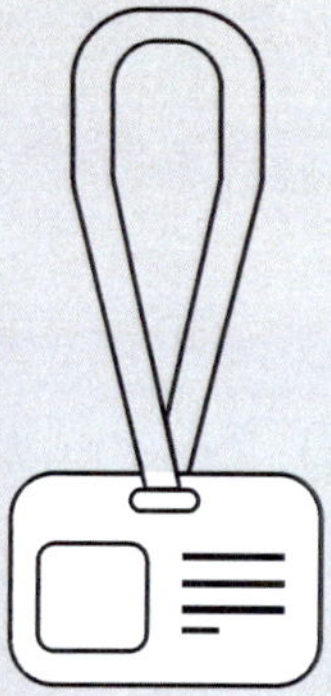

Can you style an outfit like this?

KATHERINE JOHNSON

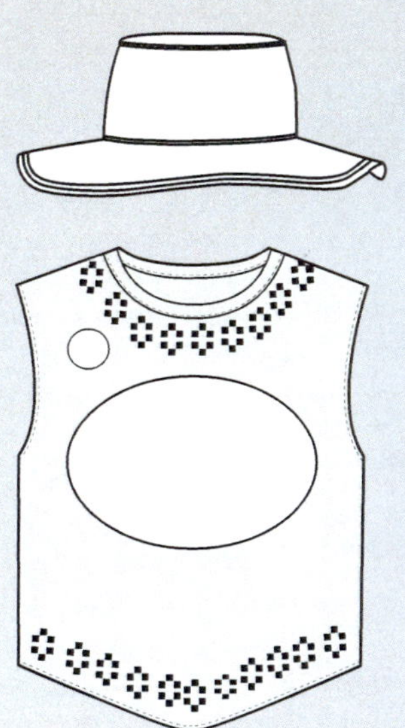

Can you style an outfit like this?

DOLORES
HUERTA

Do you love solving problems, building cool creations, or finding faster and easier ways to do everyday things? Do you ever think, *"There has to be a better way!"* You might be a future inventor in the making!

Inventors use their imagination and creativity to create new ideas that help people all around the world. What will you invent one day?

Fun Fact: Before the Garrett Morgan traffic signal, roads were a lot more dangerous! His design helped save lives by giving drivers a clear "stop, slow, and go."

Fun Fact: Marie Brown's home security system included a camera, TV monitor, and microphone — kind of like the smart doorbells we use today!

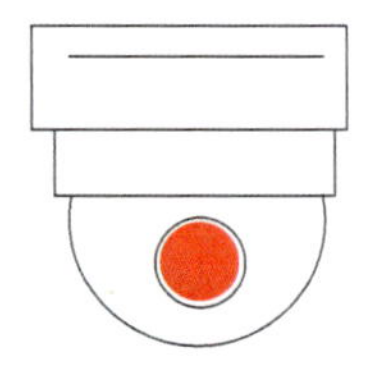

These inventors listed below created amazing things that we still use today!

CAPTCHA (2000s), reCAPTCHA (2007), and Duolingo (2011)	Luis von Ahn	Guatemalan-American entrepreneur and software developer
First Total Artificial Heart (1969)	Dr. Domingo Liotta	Argentine surgeon
Research of Yellow Fever (1881)	Carlos Juan Finlay	Cuban pidemiologist
"Arias Intensity" earthquake detector (1970)	Arturo Arias Suárez	Chilean civil engineer
X-ray Microscope (1948)	Albert Vinicio Báez	Mexican physicist
Nickel-hydrogen Battery (NiH_2 or $Ni-H_2$) for space exploration (1981)	Olga D. González-Sanabria	Puerto Rican scientist
Spin Memory Effect (2014)	Sabrina Gonzalez Pasterski	Cuban-American theoretical physicist

MORE AMAZING INVENTIONS!

Automatic Elevator Door Design (1887)	Alexander Miles	Patent No. 371,207
Early Air Conditioning Unit (1886) Carbon Filament for light bulb (1881)	Lewis latimer	Patent No. 334,078
Improved Fire Extinguisher (1872)	Thomas J. Martin	Patent No. 125,063
Mobile Refrigeration (1940)	Frederick McKinley Jones	Patent No. 132,182
Improved Ironing Board (1892)	Sarah Boone	Patent No. 473,653
Illusion Transmitter (1977)	Valerie Thomas	Patent No. 4,229761
Home Security System (1966)	Marie Van Brittan Brown	Patent No. 3,482,037
Laserphaco Probe for Cataract Treatment (1988)	Patricia Bath	Patent No. 4,744,360
Programmable Television Receiver Controller, V-Chip (1976)	Dr. Joseph N. Jackson	Patent No. 4,095,114
Three-Position Traffic Signal (1923)	Garrett Morgan	Patent No. 1,475,024
Super Soaker (1989)	Lonnie Johnson	Patent No. 4,591,071
Voice Over Internet Protocols (VoIP) (1995)	Marian Rogers Croak	Patent No. 7,599,359
Rao—Blackwell Theorem (1940s) Bayesian Statistics Textbooks (1969)	David Blackwell	Mathematical formula

Did You Know?
A patent protects an inventor's dea and makes sure they get credit for it.

Do you love drawing buildings, sketching dream houses, or imagining the tallest skyscraper in the world? You might be a future architect in the making!

Architects are creative problem-solvers who design amazing buildings and help bring them to life. They plan, sketch, and guide the construction so everything is safe, strong, and stunning.

Who knows? One day people might walk into a building YOU designed!

Architects think about questions like:
- How do people move through this building?
- Is there enough light?
- Is it safe in bad weather?
-

Architects Help the Environment
- Some architects design "green buildings" that save energy and protect the planet.

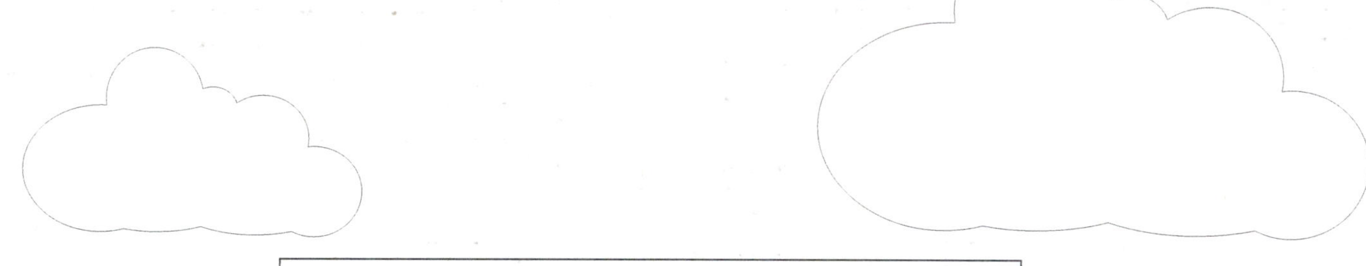

Sir David Adjaye is an architect who designs amazing buildings all around the world. He was born in Africa and grew up in different countries, which helped him see the world in creative ways. In 2000, he started his own company called Adjaye Associates, and today his team designs buildings in cities across the globe!

Fun Fact: Sir David Adjaye designed the beautiful National Museum of African American History and Culture in Washington, D.C., a place where people can learn powerful stories about history and culture.

THE NEXT LANDMARK LEADER IS...

____

(Name)

What will you be known for?

What Did This Book Teach Me About Myself?
- Two things I learned
- One goal I want to set
- One way I can be a leader

I can overcome challenges.

I am creative and full of ideas.

I use my voice to stand up for what's right.

I am becoming the best version of myself.

Page		Photographer	Image IDS
5		NASA Image Collection, Public domain	Image ID:KRJD4J
7		AFF, Steven Bergman	Image ID:2HY761B
9		IanDagnall Computing	Image ID:2EXD3P7
11		IanDagnall Computing, H. Seymour Squyer, c.1885	Image ID:2EYYHWX
13		Photo Researchers	Image ID:HRKRFW
15		GL Archive	Image ID:F63741
17		Alpha Historica	Image ID:RB16DF
19		Alpha Stock	Image ID:WR24A7
21	Alamy	PictureLux / The Hollywood Archive	Image ID:PM4J92
23		Nature and Science	Image ID:HA0CBK
25		Billy Bennight/ZUMA Press, Inc.	Image ID:2HX1B4J
27		IanDagnall Computing	Image ID:2M6RG53
29		Alpha Stock, Public domain	Image ID:2A3B0RP
31		Science History Images	Image ID:2F61N63
33		ABACAPRESS	Image ID:2FK4YD8
35		Greg Balfour Evans	Image ID:E16PRJ
37		Photo Researchers	Image ID:HRNT11

COPYRIGHT

LANDMARK LEADERS:

Trailblazers Who Shaped History

9 7 9 8 9 9 5 5 9 6 3 2 5